I0794809

THE KUDZU COOKBOOK

Cooking up a storm with that wild & crazy vine that grows in miles-per-hour!

Written by Carole Marsh Longmeyer
Illustrations by Kristen French

GALLOPADE
Bluffton Books
blufftonbooksandmore.com

Copyright 2015 Carole Marsh Longmeyer
All rights reserved

Written by Carole Marsh Longmeyer
Illustrations by Kristen French
Book design by Susan Van Denhende

Art Director: John Hanson

Janice Baker, Editor

Kathy Dean, Proofer

A Bluffton Books book

Gallopade International

Please note: Although kudzu leaves, vine tips, flowers and roots are edible, the vines are not. If you pick your own kudzu from the great outdoors, wash it carefully since it may (depending on its location) be dusty or have been sprayed with pesticides. Wear boots when harvesting kudzu, since snakes love to hide in the vines!

Other Books by Carole Marsh Longmeyer:

A Little Potty Never Hurt Nobody!

"Hello in There!"—
Poetry to Read to the Unborn Baby

Nine Months in My Mommy!—
Autobiography of an Unborn Baby

Who Ya Gonna Call?—
The Kid's Directory of Self Help

The Three Mysterious Moustachioed Mademoiselles of Le Meurice

THE KUDZU MONSTER

I've moved next to a monster,
And KUDZU is its name.
Growing is its hobby;
Eating is its game.

It ate my car for breakfast,
It ate my house for snack,
And when I go outdoors I've learned
Not to turn my back!

I have to wear my hipboots
When I go out to hang the clothes,
'Cause Monster Kudzu will sneak over
To do a taste test on my toes.

Why just today it ate a tree,
Gobbled the garage for dinner;
I can't seem to find the lawn mower,
And my dog looks like he's thinner.

Especially after it rains,
This monster acts most hungry,
So our family takes turns
Looking out for neighbor Rumley.

I know you think I'm kidding,
But I sure have a hunch . . .
That this monster known as Kudzu
Ate my kids for lunch!

What is kudzu, anyway? I've been surprised at the number of people who have never even heard the word. Either they didn't grow up, as I did, in the monstrous shadows of normal stuff transformed into gargantuan monsters of green. Or, they did, but kudzu was such a common sight they never stopped to consider that it was anything other than something to cuss. Often, kudzu was just taken for granted—both that it grew (and grew and grew) and also, that it could not be cut, sprayed, tricked, legislated, or even bombed away.

In some places kids lie on their backs in hammocks and ponder the shapes of clouds. In kudzu country, kids' imaginations toy with telephone poles that really are jolly green giants and portable grills that will vanish overnight if left beside a sneaky tendril of kudzu.

Kudzu was first brought to America around 1876 as an ornamental shade plant. Before air conditioning, the prolific vine was a welcome drape for porches and arbors, protecting shelter from swelter. On U.S. 90 in Florida, a bronze marker reads KUDZU WAS DEVELOPED HERE.

For a time, kudzu was intentionally grown as a ground cover and for forage. This was the period when the South did rise again—mean and green. By 1945 the "miracle vine" was king instead of cotton, *until* folks began to discover they had to close their windows at night to keep the kudzu from growing inside! How fast *does* kudzu grow—you measure it in miles-per-hour, some say! I, myself, have watched it grow a foot in a day.

But one country's creepy creeper is another's culinary cure-all. In Japan, *kuzu* is used in their fine cuisine as well as for highly regarded medicinal teas. Then, there's kudzu honey, kudzu cloth, kudzu cat food, kudzu paper, and kudzu clothes. (Kudzu beer and perfume are in the works, I hear!)

Kudzu has been the source and subject of clubs, legends, mail order campaigns, movies, and called both miracle and monster. But can you really eat it? Kud zu? Should you? Let's see!

Radish & Kudzu Soup

1/4 pound unsalted butter
1/2 cup finely chopped kudzu leaves
1 cup diced potatoes
1 cup white wine
1/4 cup chicken stock
1 quart half & half
Pinch of nutmeg & white pepper
1 pound thinly sliced radishes
Sour cream

In soup pot, combine butter, kudzu, potatoes, wine, stock, half & half, and seasonings and simmer until potatoes are done. Puree in food processor or blender. (Add a spoonful of flour if too watery.)

In a saucepan, bring enough water to cover the sliced radishes to a boil and cook until they are soft, about 5 minutes. Drain and add to the cream mixture.

Simmer the soup 15-20 minutes. Ladle into bright red bowls and garnish with sour cream and finely chopped kudzu leaves.

Serves 4-6 brave souls.

KUDZOOM: Speed at which kudzu grows.

Buttermilk Brownies & Frosting With Kudzu & Pecans

1 cup water
1/2 cup butter
1 cup sugar
1/2 cup vegetable oil
2 cups all-purpose flour
1/4 cup cocoa
1/2 cup buttermilk
1 teaspoon baking soda
2 eggs, beaten
Chopped pecans
Kudzu leaves, washed and dried

Combine first 3 ingredients in small saucepan; bring to boil. Combine flour, sugar and cocoa in mixing bowl; add hot mixture and stir well. Combine buttermilk and soda until soda dissolves. Add mixture and eggs to batter; mix well. Spoon into greased jellyroll pan. Bake at 400 degrees for 15 minutes. Cool and frost. Cut into squares and serve in a flat straw basket on a bed of kudzu leaves. Sprinkle chopped pecans over all. Yield: 3 and 1/2 dozen.

Frosting: Combine 1/2 cup butter, 1/3 cup buttermilk and 1/4 cup cocoa in medium saucepan and bring to boil. Add 1 box powdered sugar and 1/2 teaspoon vanilla. Blend until smooth.

In Auburn, Alabama a test field of kudzu was planted and turned under after three years. The average yield of corn later grown in the plot was 2.3 times greater than usual. Even 10 years later, the plot formerly covered in "green manure" produced an average of 9.2 more bushels per acre than nearby land!

Deep-Fried Kudzu Leaves

When using kudzu leaves, pick the tender, young leaves and avoid the older leaves and shoots which are very fibrous. Wash leaves thoroughly before using.

Dip young kudzu leaves in a thin tempura batter. Cover both sides. Deep-fry in 350 degree oil until golden brown. Drain on paper towels. Serve hot with Honey Rice.

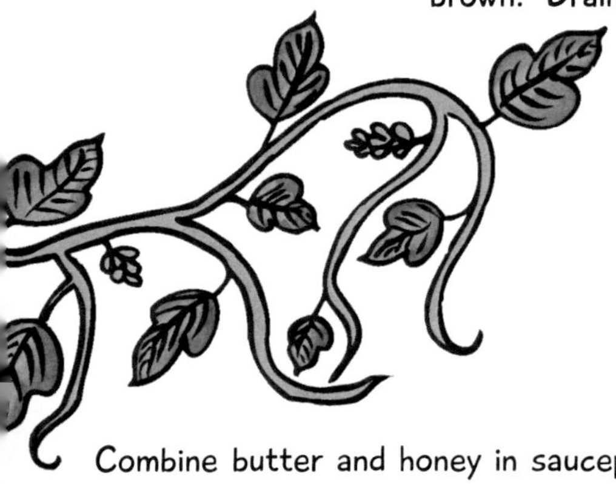

Honey Rice

4 cups hot cooked rice
1/4 cup butter
1/4 cup honey
1 teaspoon ground cinnamon
3/4 teaspoon ground ginger

Combine butter and honey in saucepan and cook over low heat until butter melts. Stir in cinnamon and ginger and pour over rice mixture and stir well.

Serve Honey Rice in shallow dish surrounded by Deep-Fried Kudzu. Chopsticks are fun. Forks are, well, forks.

Kudzu Dandelion Coffee

1 and 1/2 teaspoons roasted dandelion-root powder; purchase commercially
2 cups water
Dash of salt
1 and 1/2 teaspoons kudzu powder (see below)

Combine dandelion-root powder and water in a saucepan and bring to a boil. Simmer at least 10 minutes. Add salt and kudzu powder dissolved in 2 tablespoons water. Return to a boil and simmer for 1 minute, stirring constantly until thick. Serve hot. Serves 1 or 2. This is a rich and sweet drink.

(Kudzu powder can be purchased commercially and substituted for flour or cornstarch as a thickening agent in most recipes. Of course, you could make your own, but the recipe starts out, "Take a shovel or hoe..." so you may prefer to take the easy route, especially since home kudzu powder production is a winter activity. But just in case you care, here's how it would be made:

First, you have to dig up kudzu roots, then scrub them clean with cold water. Then you cut the clean roots into 1-inch discs. You puree these in a blender then strain. Next comes a long stretch of squeezing the liquid out of this fibrous residue.

Sooner or later you can pound the brown kudzu liquid into a bucket and let it stand for 24 hours in a cool place so the starch can settle. After you pour off the liquid that has risen to the surface, you use a knife to break up the claylike starch in the bottom of the bucket. Then do the whole thing again. And again. Finally you will end up with a pure white clay which you can cut into chunks. Let it dry for 30-40 days and you have kudzu powder. Kudzundheit!)

Why should you really use kudzu powder? A great flavor and aroma, a very smooth jelling texture, and a pretty, translucent appearance. Koromo (Japanese for "priest's robes"), or kudzu powder, dusted on vegetables before deep-frying them, produces an especially crisp, golden-brown coat, and a healthful alkalinity! If you must substitute, use 3 teaspoons flour instead of 1 teaspoon kudzu powder, or 3 teaspoons cornstarch instead of 4 and 1/2 teaspoons kudzu powder.

Of course, you and your neighbors could do like they do in Japan and treat kudzu-powder making as an entrepreneurial enterprise. The tools called for include a hoe (or a backhoe!), backpacks (gotta bring it out alive!), large wooden tubs, poles and paddles, mallets (or jackhammers) and a bamboo colander. This is their pastime of choice, similar to southern American kudzu country mud runs and moonshining, tractor pulls and pig pickin's. There are even Kudzu Festivals and a Kudzu Queen!

Strawberry Kudzu Sandwiches

Take 1 large package of cream cheese and soften. Mix in 1/2 cup of mashed ripe strawberries. Add as much confectioner's sugar as it takes to make the consistency as spreadable as you want and the flavor as sweet as you want. (Watch that you don't mash your berries so fine you have too much juice, or that you can't tell there are fresh berries in the spread.)

Cut crusts off day-old bread. (I get mine at the local discount bread store. They call it "duck bread"—for feeding to ducks at the nearby parks—and sell it for 10¢ a loaf! It's perfect for not letting any juice leak through or being so fresh that the sandwiches get squashed when you cut them.) White, sourdough or whole wheat bread are all good.

Spread bread with strawberry-cream cheese mixture and top with washed and dried fine shoots of kudzu. Cover the top slice of bread with just enough spread to help hold the sandwich together. Cut into squares, rectangles, or triangles, or use a leaf- or strawberry-shaped cookie cutter. Chill a short time to set filling.

Serve on a platter with strawberry and kudzu leaves as a centerpiece. It's especially attractive if you tint the mixture slightly with red food coloring and let the pale green shoots extend slightly from the sandwiches. Serve with Kudzu Lemonade.

In Japan, kudzu powder costs about 28¢ (U.S.) retail; in America, about $6.50 a pound.

Kudzu Lemonade

1 cup water
1 and 1/2 teaspoons kudzu powder, dissolved in 1/4 cup cold water
4 teaspoons honey
4 teaspoons lemon juice

Bring water to boil in a small saucepan. Add kudzu powder and honey. Simmer, stirring constantly, for 2 minutes or until kudzu is clear and thick. Cover, cool, and refrigerate. Stir in lemon juice when ready to serve.

Kudzu D'etat: Sudden, violent overthrow of a scarecrow!

Kudzu-cue or Open-Pit Cooked Barbecue With Kudzu

Dig a pit 3 and 1/2 feet deep. (The pit is for the pig, not the people.) Make it 1 and 1/2 feet square for small crowds (25-50 friends, relatives or neighbors) or 3 x 10 feet for large crowds (400 or so Lions, Ruraltans, Democrats, Republicans, or others). You will need a piece of sheet metal for a lid.

Start the fire 14-16 hours before you plan to eat. Use hard, dry wood and make a bed of coals 15-18 inches thick. Put a 1 and 1/2 inch layer of dry sand over the coals.

Rub the pig down with salt and lay on the sand. Cover with the sheet metal lid and put about a foot of sand or dirt on top of it. Let cook 10-12 hours. Meat can't overcook since the coals will be dying down.

When pig is done, remove from pit and place on large table laden with kudzu leaves. Mop meat down with Barbecue Sauce. Serve with more sauce, Kudzu Greens, and Kudzu Hush Puppies.

One Yankee to another:

"How'd you like your trip South? Are they as decadent as advertised?"

"Why, no. Along the highway they had nice big signs so's you'd know where you could stop and go to the bathroom."

"They did?"

"Yep. Around Virginia, they said: NICE CLEAN RESTROOMS. Then in North Carolina: RESTROOMS AHEAD. In South Carolina: STOP AHEAD FOR REST AREA."

"What'd they say in Georgia?"

"STUCKEY'S PE-CANS!"

Barbecue Sauce

2 medium onions, chopped
1/4 cup salad oil
2 tablespoons plain flour
3/4 tablespoon salt
1/2 teaspoon pepper
3 tablespoons brown sugar
1/4 cup mustard
1 cup vinegar
1 cup chicken broth
7 ounces ketchup
1 pound tomato puree
1/4 cup Worcestershire sauce

Cook onions in oil in heavy skillet. Combine dry ingredients and stir into onions. Add liquids and bring to a boil, stirring constantly. Simmer 15 minutes.

The Deep South is the area of the kudzu vine's most prolific growth anywhere in the world. It has been used to control erosion, as livestock fodder, a source of honey, an ornamental vine and a natural soil fertilizer.

Kudzu Greens

Wash kudzu leaves. Cater toward the smaller, tender leaves. Boil in a large kettle with a little salt and a tablespoon of sugar. When leaves cook down, add 1/4 cup vinegar. Continue cooking until tender. Add a few chunks of cooked pig to pot before serving.

The kudzu plant has wisteria-like flowers which smell like crushed grapes. The vine blooms in late summer. You can parboil them until tender and season with vinegar. Let stand for a day before serving your pickled kudzu flowers.

Carolina Sugar & Pepper Pie

1 partially baked 9-inch pie shell
2 cups dark brown sugar
1/4 teaspoon fresh ground black pepper
1 tablespoon flour
2 eggs
2 tablespoons melted butter
1/4 cup dark corn syrup
2 teaspoons vanilla
2 cups heavy cream (1 whipped; 1 unwhipped)

Combine sugar and flour in large bowl. Stir in eggs, butter, corn syrup, pepper, vanilla and the unwhipped cream and mix well. Pour into the pie shell.

Bake for 10 minutes at 425 degrees. Reduce to 325 degrees and bake for 40 minutes. Cool completely, then spread with the whipped cream.

Kudzone: Designated area of growth for kudzu; in other words, anywhere it wants to!

Grape Punch

1 10-ounce jar grape jelly
1 64-ounce bottle lemon-lime carbonated beverage
10 whole cloves
1 lime, sliced
1/3 cup lime juice

Combine jelly, 1 cup carbonated beverage, cloves and lime slices and juice in saucepan. Heat to boiling, stirring until jelly is dissolved. Simmer 5 minutes.

Cool, then strain to remove cloves and lime slices. Chill thoroughly, then add rest of carbonated beverage. Yield: 1/2 gallon.

Serve in a punch bowl nestled in kudzu vine. Let vine climb up bowl and extend over top edge slightly. Particularly attractive if kudzu vine is in bloom.

Creamed Fried Green Tomatoes & Kudzu

Slice green tomatoes. Dip in beaten egg, then coat with corn meal. Fry in hot oil in large skillet until crispy and brown. Drain on paper towels.

Leave approximately 2 tablespoons drippings in skillet. Add 2 tablespoons of flour and 2 cups of milk. Stir constantly to make a cream gravy. Add more milk until gravy is the consistency you prefer.

Toast English muffins and spread with butter. Lay washed and dried kudzu leaves on each open-faced muffin. Place 1-2 tomatoes on top. Cover all with gravy and sprinkle with pepper. Serve hot.

Kudz U: A university slightly south of Lizard Lick, North Carolina.

Corn Soup With Kudzu

1 tablespoon oil
1 small onion
1 and 1/2 cups fresh corn kernels
2 cups soup stock or water
1/2 teaspoon salt
4 teaspoons kudzu powder
1 and 1/2 tablespoons soy sauce
Toasted slivered almonds

Saute minced onion in large pot. Add corn, stock or water and salt. Bring to a boil then simmer on low heat for 15 minutes, stirring occasionally.

Mix in kudzu powder dissolved in 1/4 cup water. Add soy sauce and simmer until thickened. Refrigerate 6-8 hours for best flavor. Serve hot or cold. Sprinkle almonds on top of soup to serve.

Tips on cultivating kudzu:

-Choose a plot with as little dirt as possible; cement is fine.
-Plant kudzu at night when the neighbors can't see what you're up to.
-Fertilize with motor oil.
-Mulch heavily with concrete blocks.

Kudzu Gumbo

3/4 cup oil
3/4 cup flour
2 medium onions, chopped fine
8 ounces tomato sauce
3 quarts stock, any kind
1 and 1/2 bell peppers, chopped fine
2 large cloves garlic, mashed
1 tablespoon salt
1 teaspoon red pepper
2 pounds peeled crawfish
1/4 cup chopped kudzu sprouts
1/4 cup chopped green onion

Make roux with oil and flour. Add onions and cook until clear. Add tomato sauce and cook on low heat 15 minutes.

Slowly add pre-warmed stock and mix well. Add bell pepper, garlic, salt and pepper. Bring to boil and cook hard for 20 minutes. Reduce heat and simmer for 40 minutes.

Add crawfish and simmer 15 more minutes. Sprinkle with green onion and kudzu sprouts before serving.

WARNING: Don't let your cows eat kudzu (except, maybe the day before St. Patrick's Day!)

Kudzu Manju (Kudzu Dumplings in Cherry Leaves)

This traditional confection is sold in Japan in June and July. The dumpling is served like a jewel in the center of a cherry leaf wrapper.

1 cup azuki beans (a small, red bean available where you find kudzu powder)
4 and 3/4 cups water
3/4 cup brown sugar
1 teaspoon salt
9 tablespoons kudzu powder
30 cherry leaves (use kudzu leaves, if cherry unavailable)

Soak azuki beans overnight in water, then drain. Combine beans and 3 cups water in saucepan and bring to boil. Cover and simmer 50 minutes. Remove from heat and let cool for an hour.

Puree in blender until smooth and return to pan. Add salt and 1/2 cup sugar and bring just to a boil over medium heat. Simmer, stirring constantly, for 15 minutes or until thick. Uncover and cool for 1 hour. Shape into 1-inch balls.

Line a steaming tray of a large steamer with moist cotton dishtowel. Bring the steamer to a boil, then turn heat to low.

In small saucepan, combine kudzu powder, 1 and 3/4 cups water and 1/4 cup sugar and mix well. Simmer over low heat, stirring constantly until liquid turns to soft, white semisolid (but not transparent). Remove from heat and stir vigorously for 1 minute, then let cool for 1 minute.

Place a large bowl of water beside the saucepan. Spoon up about 1 and 1/2 tablespoons of the kudzu mixture. Dip your other hand into the bowl of water, then pick the kudzu off the spatula and roll into a ball and dip it into the water.

Pick up a ball of azuki paste. Put kudzu ball on top of azuki ball and pull the soft kudzu down over the azuki ball until all sides are completely covered. Seal the ball and put the dumpling, seam down, in steamer.

When all dumplings are made, put lid on steamer and steam dumplings for 7-10 minutes, until kudzu becomes transparent.

Wrap each dumpling in a cherry (or kudzu) leaf and cool or chill until firm.

Kudzu powder sold in America is imported from Japan from one of the five major shops which make the substance. Large roots are used because they are more likely to be 20-28% starch. The production of the powder is on a yearly schedule beginning in December. The process was developed in the 1200s.

Baked Sweet Georgia Vidalia Onions & Kudzu

6 large Vidalias, peeled
1 stick butter
Garlic salt
Pepper
Kudzu leaves

Slice Vidalias almost through in a + pattern. Insert pats of butter in between each section. Roll small, tender kudzu leaves into long, slender roll and insert in each section. Sprinkle all with garlic salt and pepper. Dot with more butter. Place in shallow pan filled with water about 1 inch deep. Cover with foil and bake at 350 degrees about 30 minutes, or until onions are tender. You can remove foil and sprinkle with garlic-buttered bread crumbs and continue to bake until set or slightly browned. Serve hot and steaming. Each onion serves 1-2 persons.

Tuff Snuff: Another kudzu country specialty? Valuable protein can be removed from tobacco and transformed into a gelatinous substance similar to soybean curd. (Used for making tobacco tarts?)

Sour Hot Rice

6 slices bacon
1/4 cup vinegar
Dash pepper sauce
1 medium onion, chopped
1/2 teaspoon salt
3 cups hot cooked rice

Cook bacon slowly. Drain, crumble and set aside. Pour off bacon drippings except 1 tablespoon from iron skillet. Saute onion in drippings until tender. Add vinegar, salt and pepper sauce. Blend and pour over rice. Add bacon and toss lightly. Serve with Christmas Kudzu, corn on the cob and sliced tomatoes. If you fix plates, butter corn, then sprinkle sliced hot green pepper and a splash of vinegar over all before serving.

The kudzu root can grow up to 7 feet long and weigh over 400 pounds.

Christmas Kudzu

While kudzu should grow on you (perhaps literally?!) to be a year-round favorite, here's a recipe akin to cooking any "mess of greens" that will enhance any holiday meal.

2 pounds kudzu leaves
1-2 pounds smoked meat; salty preferred
1 tablespoon sugar

Wash kudzu leaves until squeaky clean. Put in large pot with meat and sugar and cook until done. While most recipes say 30 minutes, I cook mine for a couple of hours.

When kudzu and meat are as tender as you prefer, drain and put in a bowl. Chop with a hand chopper (or use two knives) until well chopped. Drain again. Scoop some of the fat off the top of the kudzu "liquor" and mix back in with the kudzu.

Serve hot and steaming with Sour Hot Rice.

About 85% of the 750,000 pounds of kudzu powder produced in Japan each year is used to prepare their traditional confections.

Pecan Waffles

A good dish to serve late at night while you sit around listening to the kudzu grow!

2 cups all purpose flour
3 teaspoons baking powder
1/4 teaspoon salt
3/4 cup pecan meal
2 egg yolks
1 and 1/2 cups milk
6 tablespoons shortening, melted
2 egg whites

Combine dry ingredients and add pecan meal. Beat egg yolks until light. Combine with milk and melted shortening and add to dry ingredients. Mix just until smooth. Beat egg whites until stiff and fold into batter. Bake in a hot waffle iron. Makes 6-8 waffles. Serve with softened butter and warmed maple syrup. Sprinkle chopped pecans over all.

Decorate with kudzu! Anytime you need greenery, you can't get much greener than kudzu. Transplant kudzu vines into big clay pots and let tendrils sprout up trellises or across table settings. Keep well-watered. When the forks begin to disappear, you know you need to trim it back -- fast!

Kudzu Pickles

Like any "greens," kudzu is especially good with pickles. Here are a couple of pickle recipes for your kudzu kollection.

Pumpkin Pickles

1 pumpkin (about 4 lbs.)
2 and 1/4 cups sugar
2 and 1/4 cups cider vinegar
3 sticks cinnamon
15 whole cloves

Cut pumpkin into chunks. Scrape out pulp and seeds and remove rind. Cut into 1-inch squares. You should have about 6 cups of prepared pumpkin to set aside.

Combine sugar, vinegar, 3 cups water, cinnamon and cloves in a large, heavy-bottomed pan. Bring to a boil and boil gently 10 minutes. Add pumpkin pieces and boil gently 5 minutes. Remove from heat, cover and let stand 1 hour.

Return to heat and boil gently, uncovered, about 1 hour or until pieces are translucent. Turn pieces occasionally while cooking.

Pack into hot sterilized jars. Seal at once. Process 10 minutes. Makes 2-3 pints.

Dilled Green Bean Pickles

2 lbs. fresh crisp green beans
1 tablespoon salt
4 cups cider vinegar
1 cup sugar
2 tablespoons mixed pickling spice
2 cloves garlic
Fresh or dried dill

Wash beans in cool water. Snip off tops and remove strings. Leave beans whole. Soak in ice water 30 minutes. Add salt to 1 quart water and bring to a boil. Drain beans and add to hot brine. Simmer about 20 minutes, or until crisply tender. Drain thoroughly. Combine vinegar and sugar in saucepan. Tie the spices in a cheesecloth bag and add to mixture with garlic. Add beans and simmer 10 minutes. Pack beans standing upright into hot sterilized jars. Cover with hot vinegar mixture. Place a head or so of dill in top of each jar. Seal. Makes about 4 pints.

Ode to Kudzu

Crazy kudzu has caught the imagination of many a writer, especially those reared in kudzu country. James Dickey, Carl Sandburg, Flannery O'Connor, O. Henry, Thomas Wolfe, Sidney Lanier—and me: I think that I shall never see kudzu what ain't et a tree!

Kud Zoo - A zoo of cows

Fried Eels

Another thing kudzu countries seem to have in common is the common eel. They are really much tastier than you might think and were once much-loved by America's early colonists. They are still appreciated in many eastern cultures. And with squid high on the gourmet list in cuisine-trendy California, can el eel be far behind?

Skin eels (see below) and let stand in boiling water for a few minutes. Cut into 3-inch lengths. Roll in a mixture of flour and cornmeal. Pan-fry in hot fat until brown on all sides. Allow about 1/2 lb. eel for each serving. Serve hot with cooked kudzu leaves and cornbread.

To skin an eel: Cut through the skin all around just back of the head. Grasp the skin with a pair of pliers, hold the head in one hand, and pull the skin off with the other. Use a tough, hard pull to do the trick. Slit the belly from vent to throat, remove intestines and cut off head. Cut the cleaned eel into lengths for frying or chowder.

To fillet an eel: Cut cleaned eels into 6-inch lengths; chill 1 hour. With a small, very sharp knife, make a cut from the eel's back, next to the backbone, down to the rib case. Holding this cut open with the thumb, cut the fillet loose from the rib case, using a series of shallow cuts made with the point of the knife. Cut fillets into 1-inch chunks.

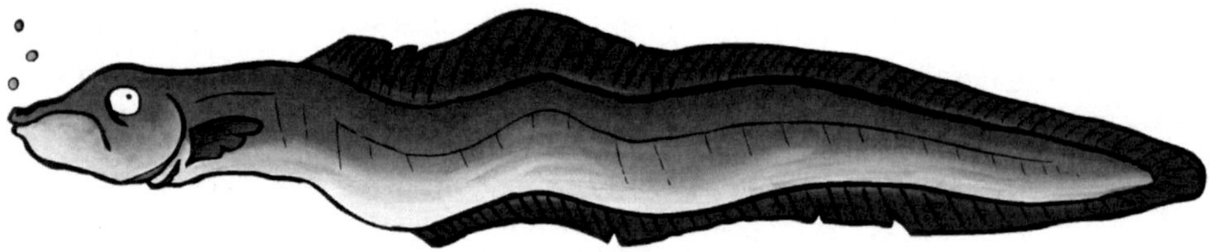

Japan invades. Far Eastern vines,
Run from the clay banks they are
Supposed to keep from eroding,
Up telephone poles,
Which rear, half out of leafage,
As though they would shriek,
Like things smothered by their own
Green, mindless, unkillable ghosts.
--From "Kudzu" by James Dickey

Kentucky Kudzu Mint Julep

(This should make James Bonds' "shaken, not stirred" martini seem right sissy!)

Version One: Klassic Kudzu Julep

Pluck kudzu sprout gently from vine just as dew of evening is about to form upon it. Rinse tenderly. Spiral the sprig in a cut glass goblet (a silver or pewter julep cup is also acceptable) being sure the top of the sprout extends "pinching" length above the top of the tumbler. Layer finely crushed ice, Kentucky bourbon and confectioner's sugar. Gently and carefully pull top of kudzu sprout up through layers to stir. Discard kudzu. What about the mint? It doesn't really add much flavor to juleps (only aroma, if your nose is close enough), but you can add it if you wish.

Version Two: Kud'n Zu's Kwickie Kudzu Julep

Take any clear, plastic glass. Snatch a kudzu leaf (as large as possible) off the vine. Do not wash. Smash down in plastic glass to cover bottom and sides. Fill with bourbon; any state or still will do. Forget ice, mint and confectioner's sugar. (The kudzu leaf is just to hide the color of the contents of the glass so you can swear to Kud'n Zu's wife, Kazandra, all y'all are drinking is health food stuff.)

Kudzu Kuntry

What's the Zip Code for kudzu?
In America, the following states are part of the
Mason-Dixon line vine's domain:
Deep in the Heart of Kudzuria: Georgia Alabama Mississippi
Covered in kudzu: North Carolina South Carolina Virginia Kentucky Tennessee Arkansas Louisiana
On the fringe:
Parts of the following states have been the targets of
the traveling tendril: (Beware points beyond!)
Maryland & southern Pennsylvania
Eastern Texas and Oklahoma
Southern Missouri, West Virginia, and Delaware
Northern Florida (including all of the panhandle)
Also sighted in: New York, Illinois, Iowa,
And reported as far north as Nova Scotia and as far west as Washington! And, Hawaii has kudzu!

Speaking of Kud'n Zu...

Shit Britches Creek* Clam and Kudzu Corn Fritters

24 cherrystone clams
1 large ear of corn on the cob
1 and 1/2 cups flour
3 eggs, separated
1 tablespoon finely chopped kudzu sprouts
1 tablespoon finely chopped tarragon
2 teaspoons baking powder
Salt and freshly ground pepper to taste
1/4 teaspoon hot pepper sauce
1/2 cup corn, peanut or vegetable oil
Sweet Red Pepper Sauce

Open clams; save juice and clams. Chop clams until coarse-fine.
Shuck corn and cut kernels from cob. In mixing bowl, put flour, chopped clams, 3/4 cup of the reserved clam liquid, corn, egg yolks, kudzu, tarragon, baking powder, salt, pepper and hot pepper sauce. Blend well.
Beat egg whites until stiff. Pour over batter and fold in.
Heat 2 tablespoons of oil in skillet. When very hot, add about 1/4 cup batter at a time, keeping each fritter separated. Add batter until skillet is filled with fritters, but not crowded.
Cook about 1 minute, or until edges start to brown before turning and cooking until brown on second side, about 1 minute. Drain on paper towels.
Add additional oil as needed for rest of fritters.
Serve hot with Sweet Red Pepper Sauce. Makes about 18 fritters.

**The name of a real creek in North Carolina's kudzu kuntry.*

Kudzu was first brought to the United States from Japan in 1876 when it was grown in the Japanese pavilion at the Philadelphia Centennial Exposition, then in 1883 at the New Orleans Expo.

Sweet Red Pepper Sauce

1 large sweet red pepper
1 small red onion
1 ripe red tomato
1 teaspoon finely chopped hot green pepper
1 tablespoon hot, spicy mustard
3 tablespoons red-wine vinegar
1/2 cup olive oil
2 teaspoons finely minced garlic
1/2 cup finely chopped kudzu

Using a long fork, hold the red pepper directly over a gas flame or close to heating element of electric broiler. Cook, turning often, so that it blisters and blackens all over. When cool enough to hold, rinse under cold tap water, peeling off burned outer skin (of pepper, not hand, hopefully!).

Cut the pepper flesh into 1-inch pieces.

Cut the onion into 1/4-inch cubes. Cut tomato into 1/2 inch cubes. Put tomato, sweet pepper, onion, hot pepper, mustard, vinegar, oil, garlic, and kudzu into food processor and blend thoroughly. Makes about 2 cups.

WHAT YOU DON'T NEED TO GROW KUDZU: Land, water, plants, cultivation, or fertilizer (Kudzu roots produce a free and continuous supply of natural fertilizer!)

Kudzu & Hominy Homestyle Breakfast

Hominy hominy does it take for this recipe? Depends on the number of folks you're expecting for breakfast. "Kudzu please pass the salt?"

1 large can hominy
Butter
Hot sauce
Salt & pepper
Kudzu leaves

Melt butter in skillet. Drain hominy and add. Add salt and pepper to taste; best light on the salt and heavy on the pepper. Serve hot. Top with hot sauce and finely minced kudzu leaves. Good with country style sausage and eggs.

Kudzu: A term of danger, as in, "Juggling them chainsaws blindfolded will kudzu good, boy!"

Red Hot Ribs & Kudzu Salad

Ribs & Braising Sauce:

4 slabs baby-back ribs, 1 and 1/4 lbs. each
4 quarts beef broth
3/4 cup red wine vinegar

Spice Mix:

1 tablespoon paprika
1 tablespoon cayenne pepper
1 and 1/2 tablespoons ground cumin
3 tablespoons Tabasco
1 and 1/2 tablespoons garlic powder
1 tablespoon ground ginger
1 cup tomato paste
1/4 cup honey
1 tablespoon salt

Barbecue Sauce:

1 cup chili sauce
1 cup ketchup
1/4 cup steak sauce
1 tablespoon Worcestershire sauce
1 tablespoon finely pressed garlic
2 tablespoons prepared horseradish
2 tablespoons dry mustard
1 tablespoon Tabasco
1 tablespoon molasses
1 tablespoon jalapeno salsa
1 tablespoon red wine vinegar

Combine braising sauce ingredients in large pot. Stir well and bring to simmer over medium heat. Add ribs and simmer until tender (almost 2 hours - but do not let meat fall off bone). Transfer ribs to flat pan. Reserve remaining sauce.

Combine spice mix ingredients in medium bowl to form a paste. Add beer if too dry.

Rub paste over ribs. Wrap each rib in aluminum foil, dull side out.

Combine barbecue sauce ingredients in medium bowl. Whisk until well-blended.

Preheat oven to 400 degrees. Cover cookie sheet with foil. Place wrapped ribs on foil, unwrap and cover with 2 cups barbecue sauce. Rewrap and bake for 10 minutes. Unwrap ribs and place on grill or under broiler to char. Serve with sauce and Kudzu Salad.

Kudzu Kahn: Founder of the Mongrel Dynasty

Kudzu Salad

Wash tender kudzu leaves, shoots and flowers. Drain well and chill. Toss with light coating of chilled barbecue sauce. Dust with sassafras. Serve cold with the hot ribs and thick slabs of homemade white bread and real butter.

Carolina Red Rice & Kudzu Chitlins*

Rice:

1/4 pound bacon
3/4 cup chopped onions
2 cups rice, cooked
2 cups canned tomatoes
1/2 teaspoon salt
1/2 teaspoon pepper
1/4 teaspoon Tabasco sauce

Cook bacon; remove from pan and crumble. Cook onions in bacon fat until tender. Add rice, tomatoes, seasonings and crumbled bacon. Cook on low heat about 35 minutes, stirring well.

**pig intestines*

Fried Chitlins:

1 package frozen chitlins
1 egg, beaten
1 cup bread crumbs, fine
Deep fat
1 teaspoon whole cloves
1 small hot pepper, chopped
1 quart boiling, salted water

Thaw chitlins in cold water. Drain and clean well. Cover with boiling salted water to which cloves and pepper have been added. Cook until tender. Drain. Cut into small pieces, dip into beaten egg, then roll in bread crumbs. Fry in deep fat until golden.

Serve rice on a bed of washed and dried kudzu leaves; sprinkle fried chitlins over top. Serve hot with giant glasses of Michael's Iced Tea.

***COMMERCIAL KUDZU:** Want to be a kudzupreneur? Sell potted kudzu to Yankee tourists for houseplants...Landscape trash dumps & auto graveyards...Start a cemetery...Create horror movie sets...*

Michael's Iced Tea

No other drink is as good with kudzu as iced tea. The following is a recipe from a 15-year-old boy. Not only is it easy and good, in spite of no real "measuring" it consistently tastes the same, which is what you want to achieve when you find the perfect tasting tea. If you discover you prefer your tea stronger, add 1-2 additional teabags.

Use automatic coffee maker. Fill with water. Put 4 teabags in pot. Let drip. Put sugar to taste in 1-gallon container and 1/2 gallon container. Divide dripped tea accordingly. Fill rest of containers with cool water. Shake until sugar is dissolved. Refrigerate. Serve over ice in tall glasses with a squirt of lemon. The large container can be for the family at dinner. The small container can be your private reserve for hanging around in the hammock.

"Let it grow." -- Jimmy Carter

Kudzu Tea

3 grams kudzu root
3 grams peony root
3 grams safflower
1 and 1/2 grams gardenia seeds
1 gram licorice

Combine ingredients with 3 cups water in teapot and simmer uncovered for about 45 minutes.

Kudzu Quiche or Kudzu & Yellow Squash With Eggs

2 cups finely chopped tender kudzu sprouts
2 cups thinly sliced yellow squash
2 tablespoons olive oil
2 cloves garlic, pressed
1 teaspoon dried leaf oregano
Red pepper flakes
4 eggs
1 cup shredded Jack cheese
2/3 cup crumbled feta cheese
3 tablespoons chopped ripe olives
2 tablespoons minced fresh parsley
2 tablespoons lemon juice

Toss kudzu and squash and saute lightly in oil with garlic, oregano and a few red pepper flakes. Do not overcook. Transfer vegetables to a lightly buttered 9-inch pie dish.

Beat eggs in bowl and stir in cheeses, olives, parsley and lemon juice. Spread over vegetables. Stir gently to combine.

Bake in preheated 350 degree oven for 20 minutes or until well set. Serves 4-6.

Kudzu Cure-Alls?

Kudzu Cream is said to be a cure all for chills, colds, diarrhea, fever, hangovers, headaches, nausea, sinus congestion, obesity, tension and sexual apathy.

Prepare Sweet Kudzu Cream by mixing 1 teaspoon of kudzu powder, 2 teaspoons of sugar and 1 tablespoon of water in a teacup with 1/2 cup of boiling water. Serve hot. Remove shoes to drink.

"Kuroyaki Chiryo Go-hyaku Shu" is a book of 500 kudzu cream remedies. Most used charred substances, ranging from plums to brown rice, salt-pickled eggplant, human hair, worms and cockroaches, mixed with the cream. It has purportedly cured many ailments since ancient times, especially since you immediately feel better so you won't have to use it. This must be the Japanese version of castor oil?!

Homemade Hot Dogs With Kudzukraut

1 and 1/2 pounds beef chuck
1 pound pork shoulder (not too lean)
3/4 pound ice
2 tablespoons plus 1 teaspoon salt
5 teaspoons corn syrup
2/3 teaspoon white pepper
1/8 teaspoon nutmeg
1/8 teaspoon ascorbic acid (vitamin C)
1/8 teaspoon sodium nitrate (saltpeter)
1/4 teaspoon liquid smoke

Grind beef and pork twice through fine blade of meat grinder, adding about half the ice with each grinding. (Or process in food processor, adding ice gradually until a smooth emulsion is achieved (about 45 seconds). Mix in remaining ingredients, stuff into sheep casings and twist into links.

Cook in water at 170 degrees for 15 minutes, or until internal temperature of the link is 155 degrees. After cooking, rinse in cold running water for 5 minutes. Chill to internal temperature of 90 degrees in ice water. Hang at room temperature for 15 minutes. Refrigerate.

To heat, place in pan of boiling water, cover and remove from heat. Let stand 5-7 minutes.

Kudzukraut

Use canned sauerkraut and heat with finely shredded kudzu leaves. Spice with hot pepper sauce. Serve over hot dogs with hot mustard.

The Kudzu Shag

Now everyone has always wondered
(Haven't you - now tell the truth!)
About the dance that's called the shag
(If you don't know it, you're short in tooth,
Or a Yankee who's never blundered
Down Myrtle Beach's Ocean Drive,
Else you'd know it's a slip-slod shuffle
That keeps pickled Southerners alive.)

Back to the story,
The legend and lore;
(If you believed the above,
You're bound to buy more.)

They say one year when the rain wouldn't end,
It washed down from the mountains and brought a friend.
A big, fat friend with long green curls
Which upon the beach did swirl
And threatened to turn the snow white sand
Into dunes the color of a garbage can.

You know the kind, that stands by the curb—
Garbage green is the only word,

To describe the can, color and beach,
Which between the bathers' toes did reach,
And tickle and trip and tease and trap,
And soon created was quite a flap:

"Green beer's ok and green beans too,
But a green, hairy beach just will not do!"
And so to the tune of "The Dock of the Bay",
The people danced and the band did play;

They pranced and squiggled and squirmed away,
Till the vine receded and the beach was saved,
And the last little tendril washed out on a wave.

Some leaves that were left were raked up in a bag,
And they named the kudzu-killing dance the Shag:
Now the state dance of South Carolina,
Where everyone says nothing could be finah,

Than to dance all night on Ocean Drive,
Get pickled and still go home alive,
To find an ambassador from Japan,
Who begs, "Export this dance --
And save our land!"

Here are a few dishes that taste especially good before or after a kudzu-kissed meal:

Hot Peppered Pecans

2 cups large pecan halves, toasted
1 cup granulated sugar
Pinch of salt
1 teaspoon cinnamon
1 teaspoon ground ginger
1/4 teaspoon nutmeg
1/4 teaspoon cream of tartar
1/4 cup water
1/2 teaspoon vanilla extract
1 and 1/4 teaspoons black pepper
Pinch white pepper
Pinch cayenne pepper

Put toasted nuts in 2 and 1/2 or 3 quart saucepan in 150-200 degree oven to keep warm.

In saucepan, mix sugar, salt, cinnamon, ginger, nutmeg, cream of tartar, peppers and water. Stir over high heat and bring to boil. Reduce heat to moderate. Insert candy thermometer and let reach 328 degrees (soft ball).

Remove from heat and add vanilla. Pour over warm pecans in warm saucepan. Stir gently until syrup turns to sugar; 2-3 minutes. Let cool and store airtight. Makes about a pound of pecans.

Peanut Butter Icebox Cookies

2 cups unsifted all-purpose flour
1/4 teaspoon baking soda
1/4 teaspoon cinnamon
1 stick unsalted butter
1/3 cup smooth peanut butter
1 teaspoon vanilla extract
1/8 teaspoon almond extract
1/3 cup granulated sugar
1/3 cup dark brown sugar
1 large egg

Sift flour, soda and cinnamon together.

In large bowl beat butter and peanut butter with electric mixer until soft and smooth. Add vanilla and almond extracts, sugars and beat thoroughly. Beat in egg. On low speed, add dry ingredients and beat 'til mixed.

Knead dough thoroughly and chill in refrigerator. Pinch off dough and roll into 1-inch balls. Put on cookie sheet. Use round-bottomed glass dipped in water (and shaken) to flatten cookies to about 1/4-inch thick. Bake at 350 degrees for about 10 minutes or until set. Let cool before removing with spatula. Makes about 4 dozen cookies. Good with Michael's Iced Tea.

"Zen Cookery" is another good source of kudzu recipes. It is published by Ignoramus Press (seriously) in Los Angeles (which explains that!).

Easy Kudzu Stir Fry

Rob fridge and freezer of everything edible and chopable. Chop meat such as chicken or pork or beef into tiny cubes. Chop or shred vegetables ranging from acorn squash to zuchinni into pieces. Almost anything, especially crunchy, will do: pickles, apples, onions. When all are prepared, use wok (If you ask, "Wok is wok?", you need the Japanese edition of this book.) or large skillet. Heat peanut oil to hot and stir fry all of the above until tender but crisp. Add Kudzu Sweet and Sour Sauce and stir until all is coated. Serve over rice with additional sauce or soy sauce.

Kudzu Sweet & Sour Sauce

1 tablespoon oil
1/2 onion
1/2 small carrot
1 green pepper
3/4 cup water
2 tablespoons soy sauce
4 teaspoons honey
2 teaspoons vinegar
1 and 1/2 teaspoons kudzu powder

Saute thinly sliced onion, chopped carrot and shredded pepper in oil in skillet. Add water, soy, honey and vinegar and boil, then simmer 3 minutes. Stir in kudzu dissolved in 1 and 1/2 teaspoons of water. Cook 1 minute, until thick. Add a splash of saki.

Kudzu Klux Klan - Secret society dedicated to the total segregation of ground covers. Known to meet after dark in national parks. Often wear green chenille bedspreads. Some run for political office (such as president of the local horticultural society); some run from police; some just have the runs.

Grilled Kudzu Corn

1/3 cup butter
2 tablespoons mustard
2 tablespoons horseradish
Kudzu leaves
1 teaspoon Worcestershire sauce
1/4 teaspoon lemon pepper
6 fresh ears corn, husks and silks removed

In small saucepan, melt butter. Stir in mustard, horseradish, Worcestershire and lemon pepper. Place each ear of corn over a set of large kudzu leaves on top of a piece of aluminum foil. Drizzle butter mixture over corn. Fold foil and kudzu leaves around corn. Grill over medium coals, turning occasionally, for about 15 minutes.

Soft-Shelled Crabs Stuffed With Kudzu

1/4 cup chopped onion
1/4 cup chopped celery
1/4 cup chopped kudzu sprout tips
2 tablespoons chopped green pepper
1 clove garlic, minced
1/4 cup melted butter
1 cup cracker crumbs
2 tablespoons milk
1 beaten egg
1/2 teaspoon dry mustard
1/2 teaspoon Worcestershire sauce
1/4 teaspoon salt
1/8 teaspoon cayenne pepper
8 soft-shell crabs, cleaned

Cook onion, celery, kudzu, green pepper and garlic in butter until tender. In medium bowl, combine mixture with crumbs, milk, egg, mustard, Worcestershire, salt and cayenne. Place crabs in shallow, well-greased baking pan. Remove top shell from crabs and fill each cavity with stuffing mixture. Replace top shell. Brush crabs with additional melted butter. Bake at 400 degrees for 15 minutes or until shells turn red and crabs brown slightly. Serves 4.

Kudzu-Fu: An ancient art of self-defense akin to carroty.

Cream of Curried Kudzu and Cauliflower Soup

1 cup ricotta cheese
1 cup milk
1 medium head cauliflower, finely chopped
2 cups chicken broth
3 cups water
1 tablespoon curry powder
1/4 cup finely chopped kudzu sprouts
1 teaspoon kudzu powder
Salt & pepper
Lemon wedges

Combine cauliflower, broth, water, kudzu, kudzu powder and curry in soup pot. Bring to boil, reduce heat and simmer, covered, until cauliflower is tender. Blend ricotta and milk until smooth. Slowly add to cauliflower and heat through, but don't boil. Add salt and pepper to taste. Serve with lemon wedges. Serves 4-6.

DESIGNER KUDZU

Look out, Kalvin Klein -- kudzu kloth may be the next haute couture. Mountain Mongols wove whole kudzu vines into everything from baskets to suspension bridges! Kudzu cloth covered the dead. (Although "Those who make kudzu cloth are too busy even to visit their friend's deathbed" is still an earnest lament of k-cloth weavers.)

Long underwear was once made from kudzu and kudzu wallpaper (grass cloth) is prized by U.S. decorators. Today, around twenty women in their sixties still harvest as much as 245 pounds of kudzu vines a day, using 52 pounds to make a single pound of finished kudzu filaments over 3-6 days of very hard work.

Kudzu cloth kimonos are still made in colors of indigo, mountain peach or safflower. The cloth can be made water-repellent with the extract made by simmering bitter persimmons in water.

Kudzu, the forerunner of Nylon, was used to make fish nets and soy sauce pressing sacks. Like many of our American folk arts, the art of making durable, beautiful kudzu cloth from the radiant, translucent fibers on hand looms is almost a thing of the past.

Kudzu Pizza

Prepare homemade pizza crust, or crust from prepared mix, or let Domino's deliver—especially if you live someplace fun like on top of a mountain only accessible by chopper or on the Outer Banks or deep in the bayou surrounded by kudzu-colored critters.

Upon crust, spread and heap: pizza sauce to which 1 tablespoon honey has been added, chopped kudzu sprouts, pecan halves (or whole peanuts, or even peanuts still in the shells), pineapple chunks (drained), and smoked ham cut into small pieces.

Top with 1 cup ricotta cheese and 8 ounces mozzarella, grated. Bake 10-12 minutes until crust is light brown. Serve hot. Good reheated for breakfast and topped with scrambled eggs or a poached egg.

Like any "salat greens," nothing is better with it than some type of corn "pone." Here are two versions to set off your more country kudzu cooking (as opposed to your more gourmet kudzu culinary efforts).

Cornbread & Milk

While some folks treat this like a "leftover" meal, try making it special for a late-night, tired, come South from Upnawth, or just got back from Disney World treat.

Bake your favorite cornbread recipe. (A moist buttermilk type with corn in it, like the recipe that follows, is especially good.) Remove from oven and slice into cubes while still warm. Put into tall glasses. Cover slowly with either ice-cold sweet milk or buttermilk. Sprinkle pepper on top and stir once with a long, iced-tea spoon.

Cush: Take leftover cornbread and break up in a skillet. While frying, add water and LOTS of black pepper until it produces a cornmeal mush. Continue to add pepper and water until the consistency of cooked grits. Be sure to use enough pepper. Eat from a thick ceramic bowl with a short spoon. Good for nothing and good with nothing, but good!

Sour Cream & Creamed Corn Cornbread

This has to be the best cornbread in the world! If you prefer yellow meal, add golden style creamed corn; if white meal, use the white creamed corn. You can leave the corn out or you can add diced pimento and green pepper and a splash of hot sauce. Learn to make without measuring and you'll find it easy to put on a pan of pone anytime. When in doubt, just be sure it's at least the consistency of a milkshake. Err on the side of runny and just bake a little longer, but the moister, the better.

Put enough oil in a heavy ovenproof skillet to well-coat bottom and sides and put in 350 degree pre-heated oven while you prepare batter. (Almost any pan of any type will do, or even a variety of muffin tins and other pans, depending upon the amount of batter you make.)

In a large mixing bowl, put almost as much self-rising corn meal or corn meal mix as you envision your selected pan(s) holding. This recipe is estimated for a 2 lb. bag. Add 1/2 cup oil, 8 ounces sour cream, 2 eggs, 1 stick melted butter, 1 can creamed corn and as much buttermilk as it takes to make the ingredients stir up into a runny milkshake consistency.

Pour into hot skillet and bake at 375 degrees until knife comes out clean.

Let cool, then run knife around edge of pan to loosen and turn out onto platter, or serve directly from pan. Because this is so moist, it does not turn out of pan as well or easily as regular, drier cornbread. You may want to cut into squares or wedges and remove with spatula.

Serve while still warm with soft, real butter.

Double-Dipped Buttermilk Batter Fried Chicken Breasts

Remove skin from plump chicken breasts, rinse off, drain and paper-towel dry. In heavy skillet, heat 1-inch cooking oil to medium-hot. Dip each chicken breast into a shallow bowl of buttermilk until well-coated, then dip into large bowl of flour until thoroughly coated. Repeat process. Fry in oil until breasts are tender and golden brown, turning often, as soon as batter has set so it will not fall off. On last turns, sprinkle with salt, pepper and minced kudzu. Drain on paper towels and serve hot with Buttermilk Gravy.

Buttermilk Gravy: Drain all but 3 tablespoons drippings from pan. Leave all fallen crust in pan. Add 3 tablespoons flour and stir into roux. Add 2 cups of milk slowly, stirring constantly over medium heat. Add 1 cup of buttermilk. Whisk during last minute of cooking. When gravy almost reaches thickness desired, remove from heat and continue to stir-whisk. Serve over creamed potatoes or homemade biscuits with chicken and kudzu greens.

Kudzu Pasta

Now you can say, "Hey, 'at's Italian!" about kudzu. One of the most popular ways to use kudzu powder is to make noodles or kudzu-kiri. While these can only be bought in specialty stores in America (and at the local grocers in Japan), you can also make your own.

Originating during the 1200s, kudzu noodles have been used in Zen Temple Cookery, so they're bound to spice up a Baptist church supper. While they look like spaghetti, they are especially smooth of texture and light in flavor.

Homemade Kudzu Noodles

6 tablespoons kudzu powder
1 and 1/2 cups water

In a small saucepan, dissolve kudzu powder in 1 and 1/2 cups water and bring to a boil. Simmer, stirring constantly to keep from sticking to bottom of pan. Cook 4-5 minutes until kudzu is very thick and clear. Spoon into moistened 9-inch square baking dish. Smooth out with a spatula. Set pan in ice water to cool quickly.

Carefully lift jelled kudzu from sides of pan. Invert pan over moistened cutting board. Moisten top of sheet of kudzu then slice into thin noodle strips by pressing a moistened knife down into the sheet. (Re-wet knife for each cut.) Prepare and serve immediately, or put in bowl of ice water to hold.

Kudzu Noodles With Vegetables & Sesame Dressing

2 fresh mushrooms, sliced very thin
1/2 cucumber, thinly sliced
1 hardboiled egg, sliced very thin
1/4 cup slivers of red bell pepper
1/4 cup bean sprouts
1/4 cup slivered almonds
2 servings kudzu noodles

Arrange noodles on plate and top with above ingredients. Serve with dressing made with: 1/4 cup soy sauce, 1/4 cup oil, 1/4 cup honey, 1 tablespoon hot mustard, 1/4 cup vinegar, 1 tablespoon sesame seeds.

Kudzu Noodles With Fruit & Molasses Yogurt

Large chunks of ice
4 servings kudzu noodles, chilled
1 apple, sliced very thin
1 banana, thinly sliced
1 pear, sliced very thin
1 cup thinly sliced green melon
1 cup thinly sliced orange melon
Chilled molasses
Yogurt
Raisins

To prepare: Chill all ingredients. Place chunks of ice in individual serving bowls. Lay chilled noodles on top. On top of one side of noodles place fruits. On other side, place melons. Top fruits with chilled molasses. Top melons with yogurt mixed with a small amount of molasses. Sprinkle raisins over all. Serve with chopsticks.

In 1902, David Fairchild, author of "The World Was My Garden," had a kudzu brainstorm. He decided to plant kudzu seedlings around his home in Washington, D.C. "They all took root with a vengeance," he reported, "and grew over the bushes and climbed the pines, smothering them with a mass of vegetation which bent them to the ground and became an awful tangled nuisance." For years, he tried to undo what he had so innocently done -- but to no avail. In 1938, he issued warnings to others. But it was too late!

When Dr. Fairchild later served in Japan as a plant explorer for the U.S. Department of Agriculture (no kidding; served him right, didn't it?!), he saw the possibility of using kudzu as the Japanese did: as livestock pasturage, hay and fodder. Later, kudzu seeds were available through mail order catalogues and folks followed Dr. Fairchild's advice, just in case you're wondering how the wild weed came to wreak havoc along our Interstate Highway System!

Manyoshu is a book of poetry compiled around 600 A.D., which has the first mention of the kudzu vine.

Kudzu Kookies (Kudzies) for the Kids

Kids love kudzu! For them, it's a hundred million hiding places, a challenge to outsmart snakes you can't see, thick, gnarled vines to swing over creek gorges on, and an endless source of tall tales to scare younger brother and sister with! Treat kids to a vine full of these simple sugar cookies (which should be monstrous in size, of course!)

1 and 1/2 cup sifted confectioners sugar
1 cup butter
1 egg
1 teaspoon vanilla
1/2 teaspoon almond flavoring
2 and 1/2 cups flour
1 teaspoon soda
1 teaspoon cream of tartar

Mix sugar and butter, then mix in egg and flavorings. Blend dry ingredients in and refrigerate 2-3 hours. Roll dough on floured pastry cloth. Cut with any large, leaf-shape cookie cutter. Sprinkle with sugar and bake on lightly greased cookie sheet 7-8 minutes. If available, stretch kudzu vine on table and place cookies for afterschool plucking! Makes around 4 dozen large cookies.

Southern Kudzu Lore: Snakes don't get in kudzu. Why? Because it tickles them!

Kudzucchini Pie

Pie shell
2 and 1/2 cups pureed cooked zucchini
1 cup half and half
1 and 1/2 tablespoons kudzu powder
1/2 cup honey
1 teaspoon cinnamon
1/2 teaspoon powdered gingerroot

Combine pureed zucchini with other ingredients and mix until smooth. Fill shell and bake for 15 minutes at 450 degrees. Reduce temperature to 300 degrees and bake for 45 additional minutes.

HAVE A KUDZU PARTY!

1. All kudzu cuisine
2. Decorate with kudzu
3. Prize (potted kudzu) for the best kudzu costume
4. Do the Kudzu Shag!
5. Tell kudzu jokes
6. Have a kudzu trivia contest, "Jeopardy" style!

Kan't get enough kudzu? Here are some more kudzu facts and humor:

While in kudzu country we just have to step outdoors to gather kudzu (or leave the door open for a while). In Japan, obtaining the roots of wild kudzu is hard work and expensive. During the cold winter months from December through March, the Japanese hike as far as 2-3 miles into the mountains to search for the valuable vine. After digging the long, tangled roots out of the underbrush with a hoe, they hack them into 3-foot lengths and backpack them in burdensome bundles.

OTHER NAMES FOR KUDZU (that can be repeated!): Kuzu (Japan) White Gold (the root/powder) Green Menace Green Manure

Kudzoo: A musical instrument played by members of the Chocowinity Philharmonic Orchestra.

The perfect Kudzert after a truly gourmet country kudzu meal is the Moon Pie. (C'mon, I dare you: Serve on a silver tray at your next dinner party!)

The Japanese put the kudzu root through a 16-day washing to achieve a final pure, white clay from which kudzu powder is made. While the less refined but grayer kudzu powder is supposed to have more nutrients (like unrefined grain for breads), the Japanese prize the white-white powder much as they do white bread.

While we curse our kudzu, in Japan, chlorophyll is extracted from kudzu leaves and sold commercially on a large scale.

IN JAPAN, KUDZU IS RENOWNED AS ONE OF THE "SEVEN AUTUMN FLOWERS."

YOUR KUDZU LIBRARY

Want to curl up in the corner and read a good book groundcover to groundcover? Try these! They really exist!!

A Barefoot Doctor's Manual, U.S. Department of Health, Education and Welfare, 1974

The Vine That Ate The South, Georgia, 1973

How Kudzu Conquered the South, *Miami Herald*, 1976

Front Porch Farmer, 1949 (Was a bestseller that made kudzu famous!)

Be Very Cautious With Kudzu!, *Country Life*

Landscaping With Kudzu, Macmillan, 1959 (A "Northern" publisher, of course!)

Kudzu Is This (Former) Farmer's Friend, E. M. Rowalt, 1936

Zero to Thirty Million Mile-A-Minute Seedlings, 1941

Rise & Decline (& Re-rise) of the Miracle Vine, 1973

+ WKUD-TV presents:

KUDZU: A film produced with a grant from the National Endowment for the Arts. Nominated for an Academy Award!

KUDZU CLOTH: A silent documentary (What can I say?!)

The "K" Word: A Kudzu Klossary

Kabu - Small heart-shaped, pure-white turnips that have a mild, slightly sweet flavor

Kakkon - Dried diced cubes of kudzu root

Kanten - Agar, or a sea vegetable gelatin sold in flakes, bars, strands or powder

Katakuriko - Cooking starch made from the roots of the dog-tooth violet

Kinako - Roasted soy flour

Koko - Grain coffee

Kombu - A Japanese sea vegetable similar to kelp, used in soups and stews

FOR SALE:

Kudzu seeds, root extract and powder are available via various suppliers at alibaba.com.

Organic kudzu root power, supplements and other products are available via amazon.com.

Eden organic kudzu root starch is available from iHerb.com.

Kudzu Porter, a beer, is available from Back Forty Beer Co.

Kudzu root tea is available from Tea Haven.

Table linens made from kudzu are available from Dancing With Kudzu in Lakemont, Georgia, which also hosts workshops on kudzu fiber-processing for weavers, knitters, papermakers and other artists.

Kudzu Kabin Designs: Nancy Basket's shop in Walhalla, South Carolina sells lampshades, baskets, folk art and other items made from kudzu.

You can find kudzu fragrance candle- and soap-making supplies on eBay.com.

Find kudzu blossom jelly at alabamasunshine.com, wildpantry.com, old-mill.com.

PLEASE POST IN YOUR KUDZU KUNTRY KITCHEN!:

CAUTION
COOK FAST!*

*Or your home may wind up on the botanical tour!

& always remember...WHILE YOU SLEEP: KUDZU DOTH CREEP!

Carole Marsh is a native of Marietta, Georgia. She has also lived in Louisville, Kentucky, Greenville, South Carolina, and Tryon and Rocky Mount, North Carolina- great kudzu places, all! She wrote this book when she lived in Bath, North Carolina, next door to a large patch of kudzu planted for privacy over a pirate tavern, and wondered if Blackbeard's treasure hid beneath.

Kristen French is a native of Gretna, Nebraska and has been raised in the Midwest her entire life, too far north for even the mighty kudzu to survive. She only discovered it when traveling down south for college in Savannah, Georgia, where she became an eyewitness herself to the strength of such a vivacious plant.

Susan Van Denhende was born and raised in the South- too far south to have heard of kudzu, apparently. Kudzu is as much of a mystery to her as the fact that one can live too far south to be in the South. Based on this book, she expects that it is as hardy and fast spreading as bamboo, so she hopes she never has to fight kudzu for possession of her lawn. It is surely a battle she would lose.